Getting Kids to Write!

A Natural Approach to Creative Writing

Written by Greta Barclay Lipson, Ed.D.

Illustrated by Dan Grossmann

Teaching & Learning Company

1204 Buchanan St., P.O. Box 10
Carthage, IL 62321-0010

Cover photo by Images and More Photography

Teaching & Learning Company
1204 Buchanan St., P.O. Box 10
Carthage, IL 62321-0010

This book belongs to

_____

Dedication
For Douglass and Sherry Campbell,
In praise of: laughter (frequent and hearty),
the love of friends (tested over time)
and the ineffable kindness of fate
(that brought us together)!

Table of

TLC10213 Copyright © Teaching & Learning Company, Carthage, IL 62321-0010

Contents

Dear Teacher or Parent,

The instructional approach to writing, in this book, is informal and derives from a spontaneous framework. We use language as a natural process, and the activities here allow for many opportunities to practice writing easily from personal experience, from the senses and from our desire to communicate.

You have heard this many times before, but I am going to repeat it with zealous conviction: If you want your students to learn to write—then you must have them write and write and write! You must also encourage them to read (or read to them) in order to appreciate the great variety of written forms and styles.

As babies we learn to speak without benefit of formal instruction. In the same way we can learn to write our letters, our personal stories, reflections and opinions! Language comes to us first as a free-flowing experience rather than a form of academic rules and strictures. We learn to speak through a long series of trial and error experiments—from our environment, from the level of need and from our appreciation for the spoken word.

First, let's generate writing skills by providing all manner of ideas! Release the student to produce a body of work first! Get the motion going. Honor the process! Respect the product. Keep your expectations reasonable. Your classroom is not the newsroom of *The New York Times*! Of course we want our students to know about spelling, structure and grammar—but not as an initial impediment to a free flow of ideas! Refinement can wait.*

My first significant experience with this "naturalistic" approach, rather than classic, was in a college freshman class where the teacher (a former hard-hat construction worker and a graduate of Princeton) assigned three papers a week, one page each, on any topic! Great moans rent the air until he promised that he would not mark down for anything! He would only comment on the interest level of the papers.

We could fulfill the assignment by writing a paragraph describing a dream, a wish, a conversation, a poem, a story, an experience, an emotion, a fantasy . . . . Almost anything would do as long as it imparted an interesting idea!

This was quite new to us! Though we kept up the drumbeat of despair and groaned with pain—the novelty was appealing. We wrote and wrote and wrote—about whatever moved us, and it truly became easier. Finally we were told that our writing style had changed from stuff that was rigid, self-conscious and formal to papers that were relaxed, warm and human!

That "freeing" experience inspired me to follow informal guidelines in creative writing with my own students forever after. This is my invitation to other like-minded teachers.

Use this book however it serves you best! **Liberate that writing spirit!** I know you can do it!

Sincerely,

Greta

Greta Barclay Lipson, Ed.D.

---

*For a more definitive philosophical view, see *Teaching the Universe of Discourse: Language Arts, English Language, Composition and Exercises,* by James Moffett, Reprint 1987, Boynton-Cook Publishing, Upper Monclair, NJ.

What's Included

This book . . .

1. Gives examples of writing for suggested topics.

2. Provides ideas for discussion preliminary to writing.

3. Encourages ongoing, student-generated ideas.

4. Features a great range of writing opportunities.

5. Emphasizes personal experience as source material.

6. Illustrates that writing, like speaking, is communication.

7. Creates an informal framework for writing efforts.

8. Views all writing as a creative endeavor.*

9. Demystifies the dynamics of writing.

10. Points up the qualitative difference between the spoken and the written word.

*Just as we all have different styles of speaking—so have we different styles of writing. The choices of words, mood and structure are all creative choices, whether they be bland or colorful, primitive or refined.

Attention, Teachers

The examples in this book are simply suggestions. Do what serves the writing process best in your class. If your students want to conform and start the assignment by using the suggested opener:

"I was scared silly when . . ."

that is acceptable. But if some of your young authors prefer to begin the topic in other ways, that is fine! If the account of a real experience mutates into a fictional account that is fine, too. The building materials are words and ideas, so trust the dynamics of the process.

Whichever way your students find their muse, their inspiration or their guiding spirit–when they begin to understand the power of words, you've done your job well.

To Start

What Is This Book About?

This book is about writing, creativity, examples, story starters, themes, clues to beginnings, offshoots (real and imagined) and endings! It is about modeling the writing process with good, understandable examples to be found throughout this book. It is also about an unfettered classroom atmosphere and easy-going practice in writing!

Use Your Own Experience

We are often told when writing that we should always use our own experience and background and not try to create a landscape that is totally foreign to us. In this way we have true-to-life subject matter upon which we can easily expand. If you live on a farm, you will know and understand the rhythm of daily living, the fun, the danger and the problems better than someone who lives in urban Detroit! If you live near an ocean, a desert or mountains, your experience is a revelation to someone who lives on the plains of Kansas or in the heart of bustling Manhattan.

That Reminds Me!

The difficulty in writing is that even though our lives are filled with the substance of engaging stories, it is hard to summon up material on command! But there are indeed experiences which are common to all of us which we can recapture and use. We are able to resonate to the topic. We are talking about the " . . . that reminds me" reaction. "If you think you had a crazy dream—just listen to mine!" These topics have a commonality because the theme evokes our personal memories! Most of us have grandmas, grandpas, aunts, uncles and cousins. The cast of characters is similar but, oh, how unalike the individuals are!

Purposeful Writing

To the Teacher

Purposeful writing means that what is written is for an authentic reason—as in writing letters with the expectation of receiving an answer!

Author's Note

When I was in middle school (far back in the ancient past) we had a school foreign exchange letter program in which I participated. Everything about the experience was fascinating. My correspondents were Serena Pugh and Selwyn Marks who lived in Great Britain. Even their names were intriguing as was the curious handwriting, the sometimes mysterious idiom, the formality, and finally their respective descriptions of the city of Manchester, England, across the Atlantic Ocean, roughly 4000 miles away!

Assignment

This Makes a Great Hall Display!

Write a letter to a well-known person and ask what his or her favorite book was as a teenager and what made it special! Your choice of correspondent might be a children's author, a political figure, a prominent business person, a journalist, an artist, a musician or a sports figure. You pick the recipient of your letter! Be careful not to overwhelm one single person with more than one written inquiry. Each student in the class must choose a different individual. As a courtesy, you may enclose a stamped, self-addressed envelope along with your letter. Make certain that your name and address are legible.

Another Idea

Your entire class may decide to write one single class letter to an author who is particularly popular with everyone. In that case, compose a letter with just a few questions from the class. Decide carefully about the interesting points of inquiry. In this way the reply will be addressed to the entire class and will be a truly exciting experience.

For the Teacher

Robert Cormier (the author of *The Chocolate War, I Am the Cheese, Tunes for Bears to Dance To* and many more books) was asked the serious question, "What made you become a writer?" His reply was that when he was in middle school, his teacher handed back his English paper and said emphatically, "Robert *you are* a writer!"

She didn't say, "That was a nice paper." or "Good report." Instead she said, " . . . you are a good writer!" and those words truly inspired him to follow his interests and become a professional writer.

Purposeful Writing

Write a letter to a famous person in public life who interests you. Tell something about yourself as an introduction in your letter. What single question would you like to ask him or her? (Remember, it is impolite to ask questions about money.)

What's Creative?

The root word for *creative* is *create*. Look in your dictionary for the definition of the word. In my *American Heritage Dictionary* it says: "To cause to exist, to bring into being, to produce things through artistic or imaginative effort." In its way, all writing is creative. You choose the words. The sentences are constructed by you. The flow of language comes from your style of expression.

When you are creative, it can mean that you . . .

made suggestions for a project

built a tree house

invented a new game

built a car out of a wooden orange crate

baked a cake

arranged flowers in a vase

wrote a song

made a tool kit

made a tin can telephone

made a Jacob's ladder

wove a vest

told a story

composed a silly song

wrote a poem

painted a picture

played a musical instrument

dreamed up a school book sale to raise money

put together a great sandwich

named your dog

made a soap sculpture

planted seeds and watched over them as they grew

carved out a pumpkin for Halloween

choreographed a dance for a program

built and painted scenery for a play

made a clothespin animal to hold notes

designed an advertisement

put together a model plane

wrote a story

baked a pizza

thought up a slogan

designed a geometric pattern

said something funny

dreamed up a great simile and/or metaphor

made a sock puppet

made peanut brittle

trained your dog to do a trick

The reason for all of this is to remind you just how creative you are (or can be) almost every day, without realizing that so much of what you produce is inventive! Considering this new understanding of being creative, contribute to a list of activities on the chalkboard that you think are creative efforts.

What's Creative?

Assignment

Who would think that you could do something creative with your address? Well it can be done with the following directions: Each numeral of the address will equal the number of syllables for each line. A zero will allow you to use as many syllables as you choose. To count syllables correctly, beat out the rhythm as you say the words or clap the syllables. All the lines put together must make sense. The street name must be *your* name. You may use other addresses, too.

24570 Eckhardt

2 Hi there,
4 mystery kid.
5 With the great big smile
7 Come over and say, "Hello."
0 I would like to know you better!

by Jill Eckhardt

647 Alexander

6 I can't let summer go.
4 It makes me sad.
7 To say good-bye to freedom.

by Jay Alexander

15733 Haydu

1 Plop!
5 The limp pizza fell
7 On the messy kitchen floor.
3 Here, doggie
3 Problem solved.

by Karen Haydu

What Is Creative?

Describe something very creative which you have either produced or seen or heard.

What's Creative?

The Value of a Journal!

Once, when I was talking to a group of school kids, a 12-year-old girl asked a question that writers hear all the time: "Where do you get your ideas?"

I answered honestly that most of my ideas come from experiences both good and bad, from reading newspapers, from listening to the radio and TV and from what is ordinary or weird around us! My suggestion to her turned out to be something I wish someone had told me–and that is– if you are interested in writing, *keep a journal* in which you record all the funny, sad, everyday things that you experience or read about. These events may not seem very important to you when they happen, but later they may contain the kernel of an idea which you can expand!

When you consider keeping a journal, think of yourself as a photographer recording word pictures of daily events. Do not think diary! Do not think about highly personal or secret feelings. Think of yourself as an alert reporter for your local newspaper with eyes and ears on your world. You will be gathering raw material for your writing, and it will be your own rich treasure chest.

You may think that your life is not very colorful and nothing much happens, but that isn't true! There are many events in your day which, as you retell them, begin to take the form of an interesting anecdote which may entertain a listening or a reading audience. And now and then a true story moves and changes inside your head–with a new way of looking at things and you create your own situations in a literary effort!

Real-life incidents may start out as mundane (ordinary) and can easily become the stuff of fictional stories. Ask the question, "What if this or that happened differently? Or what extraordinary things could happen in an ordinary situation? Then what?" Give the writer in you a chance to move toward your outer limits and the infinite capacity of your mind.

And finally, to your surprise, there may be a story that happens inside your head–part true, part made up–from your very own observations and/or imagination. If you discover such power, that is another wonderful source that can help you write.

Name _____

The Value of a Journal!

Design a colorful and attractive cover for your idea journal. Make it loud and inventive. You may use a loose leaf, or any other notebook, that will be tough enough to last. Cut out the wildest pictures, use vivid markers, brilliant colors and dazzling items to decorate the cover. Start today! It will be part of your writer's magic!

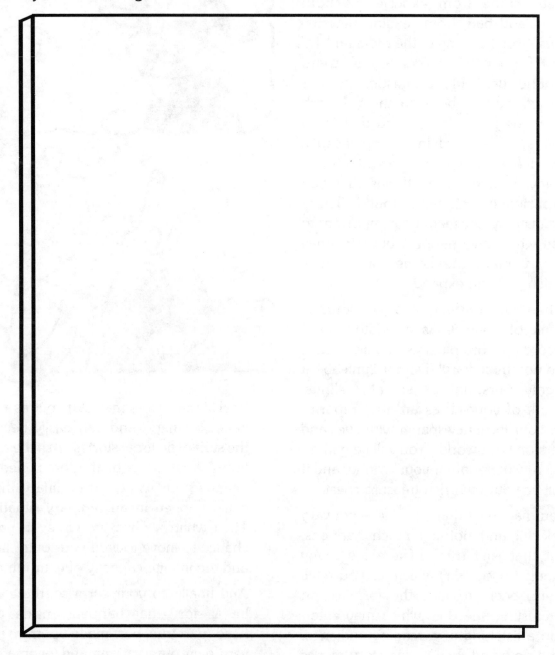

P.S. I do this, too!

Why Do People Write?

Class Question

How would you answer the question "Why do people write"? List on the chalkboard as many different replies as the class can think of!

People Write To . . .

communicate with others
share good feelings
say "thank you"
sort out bad feelings
inform
convince
persuade
express gratitude
recount personal experiences
express love
spread hate
enjoy the power of words
express emotion

defend a belief or a point of view
defend an ideal
entertain
make people think
impress
conduct business and commerce
create literature and poetry
rally for a cause
make people laugh or cry
apologize
sell
solicit money
reveal history

How Is Writing Different Than Speaking?

Written language can be richer and more expressive than the spoken word. The writer can choose each word carefully and more sensitively in a written message. The best part of writing is that you can re-write, change things and find just the right words. The next best part of a letter, a note, an article or written material is that the reader can read and reread every word. This is a special treat if the writer has had special things to say that appeal to you! Writing in newspapers, magazines and books reaches a vast audience and enjoys a very long life. (On a personal level, it is often easier to write serious things than it is to say them face-to-face.)

There are many kinds of writing among which are . . .

Expository writing explains
Narrative writing tells a story
Persuasive writing tries to convince

The hardest part of writing is having to rewrite and make several (or more) drafts! There is not a writer alive who doesn't have to change what he or she has written. When professional writers put words on paper it is then given over to an editor who reads the material to see if it is clear and understandable. This is true for people who write newspapers, books, drama, poetry and certainly technical writing. Accepting criticism isn't always easy but, as in all things, it helps writers improve their craft!

Example

Why do I write? I write because it makes me so happy. It makes me soar. When I put the pen on the paper, I am flooded with ideas and inspiration. When I win a writing contest it makes me proud of myself and builds my self-confidence. When I lose, it just makes me want to write even more. Writing is an outlet for my feelings. When I am in a fight with a friend, writing a fictional story about it helps me cool down and sometimes even resolves the problem. I reach down deep in myself and find all the anger buried there, and often a solution with it! That's the power of the pen!

Emily Dworkin, age 12

Collective Assignment

Ask the students to bring in greeting cards. When the collection is adequate, the cards may be used to cut and paste for each student's own design and written message! These customized designs and sentiments are highly personalized and one of a kind!

Decide who the card is for. Write a short message in the card to let that person know that you appreciate him or her. Make it sincere and thoughtful. Here are some suggestions to expand upon:

- I am so lucky that you are my (friend, grandparent, brother, sister, teacher).
- Every day I think of you and your smiling face.
- Your kindness means so much to me.
- Thank you for giving me so much (courage, hope, inspiration . . .).
- You have taught me how to be (forgiving, brave, understanding . . .).
- No one I know can take your place in my world.
- You make the sun shine, the sky blue and the air sweet.
- With a friend like you I never have to envy anyone.
- You are a gift to your students (family, neighborhood, church . . .).
- When you are around, the sun shines and the flowers bloom.
- It is hard to say this face to face, but I think you are the greatest.
- I am grateful for all the good times and friendship we share.
- What a great favor you did for my family. You make kindness look so easy.
- Thank you, thank you–for helping me when I was under a dark cloud.
- I needed help and you were there, as always, to support me and give me a real boost.
- You are a team player and we all appreciate your hard work.
- It has been tough for you, but I thank you for your honesty and courage.

Why Do People Write?

How do you feel about writing? Be honest and express your true feelings, good or bad!

Writing Topics

To the Teacher

It is good practice to have a group or class discussion about any given topic. It helps to explore a writing subject from different viewpoints; it suggests offbeat avenues; it encourages divergent thinking and it provides a segue into the written word!

Discussion

Select any topic on the following list for discussion before writing. Try to inspire different perspectives and points of view.

Keep the List Growing

1. I Would (Like/Not Like) to Be Famous
2. When I Got Lost
3. My Best Friend
4. Caught in a Lie
5. I Should Have Kept My Mouth Shut
6. An Embarrassing Moment
7. If I Could Go Back in Time
8. A Song I Love Because
9. The (Best/Worst) Movie
10. A Great Experience
11. A Gift I Couldn't Stand
12. My Favorite Musical Group
13. Hanging Out at the Mall
14. This Is the Way I Feel About Sports
15. My Idea of a Hero Is . . .
16. I Like People Who . . .
17. A Vacation with the Family Is
18. When I See Someone Out of Control, I . . .
19. If I Could Make a Wish
20. If I Could Be Someone Else
21. I (Love/Hate) Dancing
22. Pets Are Good for People Because
23. A Bad Argument Happened When
24. What Makes Me Happy?
25. When I Am Down, I . . .
26. Clothes I Think Are Weird
27. What Compliment I Would Like
28. My Favorite Dish Is . . .
29. My Best Moment Was
30. I Think That You Must Keep a Promise Because
31. A Friend I Would Like
32. My Future Car Will Be
33. If the Principal Would Listen
34. If I Could Live in a Different Time, It Would Be . . .
35. If I Could Be Anything I Wanted to Be . . .
36. Dear Editor of the School Paper, I Have a Complaint
37. When My Friends and I Made a Bad Decision
38. I (Love/Hate) Junk Food
39. I Had to Say "I'm Sorry"
40. The Most Nervous I've Ever Been
41. The "In Crowd" in My School Is . . .
42. A Poem to a Special Person
43. Report Card Day Is . . .
44. On the Last Day of School . . .
45. When I Get Test Jitters
46. I Hate It When That Happens
47. When I Almost Got into Serious Trouble
48. My Most Outstanding Characteristic
49. I Am (Am Not) a Sports Freak!
50. I Would Like to Talk with . . .

To the Teacher

Here is another approach to writing using divergent thinking: Select a word which you think is evocative of corollary words, thoughts and impressions such as:

Nouns: A Person, Place or Thing

Mother	Pizza
Dad	Dance
Grandparents	Halloween
Dentist	Candy Floss
Neighbors	Computer
School	Movies
Vacation	Christmas
Lifeguard	Red
Baseball	Crybaby
Birthday	Hockey

- Ask for one word and write it in the central position on the board! We will call this the "kernel" word.

- Ask the class for words that come to mind when they react to the kernel word.

- If a person contributes the word *red*, it may remind someone else of "cars" which may be mindful of "traffic ticket" which may also remind someone of "hot dog!"

- If a response seems "way out," ask the person who volunteered to explain that particular connection. It can be a fascinating look into the circuitry of the human mind.

For Example

What exactly does a hot dog have to do with a traffic ticket? The answer may be that in some places a reckless, crazy driver is called a hot dog! And so it goes with the power of words. Our reaction to words has the imprint of our own experience–be it bland, good, bad or wild.

Assignment

Make your own web. Enter as many divergent thoughts as the kernel word produces in your head. Make some connections of these thoughts and build your own quirky story. Exchange your kernel word with a partner. Compare and contrast your partner's divergent thoughts with yours.

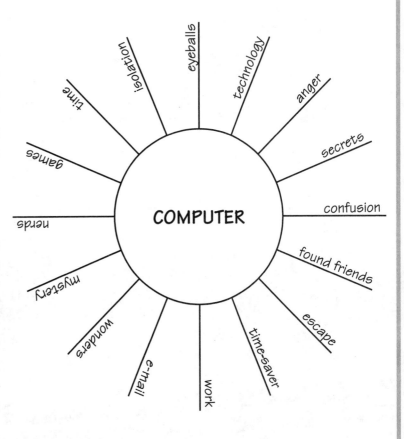

Writing Topics

This is your chance to choose one subject among the 50 listed topics at the beginning of this section. Pick one which you find easy to write about. It can be funny, sad, ordinary or grumpy. Write a paragraph or more.

Topic: _____

You Explain the Picture

This assignment is about your reactions! Many of us, when looking through the papers, smile privately at some pictures because they tickle our funny bone or say something to us. Look through magazines, newspapers or advertising flyers. Find a good, large picture which deals with a subject that you respond to. It can be serious, beautiful or comical and/or it may remind you of a person or a situation.

- Perhaps it is a color picture of a motorcycle, and in your dreams you would want to own one when you are old enough.
- Maybe it is a picture of a soaring mountain peak in all its glory, and you love the outdoors and the idea of camping.
- Do you want to learn to fly and pilot a passenger plane?
- Would you like to be a famous musician who performs in front of large audiences?
- Does a family trip to an amusement park thrill you?

Assignment

1. Find the picture that has creative possibilities.
2. Paste the picture at the top of a large piece of construction paper.
3. Write your personal reactions in a paragraph. Explain what the picture means to you.
4. Paste your remarks beneath the picture.

If you were to see a picture of a thrilling basketball game, you may yearn to be there, or be the star, or think of a really tall kid in your class or be the sports announcer! There is no telling what a picture says to any one person! Advertisements and major news photos are designed to make people pause and capture the focused interest of the reader.

Name _____

You Explain the Picture

In our family we make magazine birthday books. This means we cut out all kinds of pictures that we think suggest something funny (and kind!) about the birthday person! We write a line underneath each picture to help explain it and help things along. Our favorite in *Grandma's Birthday Book* is a picture of a wrestling match. Underneath it says: "Grams has a quiet evening out with her friends." Find a picture and write a caption for someone in your family.

I Was Scared Silly

Sometimes there are events in our lives that scare us so completely that we never ever forget them no matter how much time goes by! If you have had a frightening experience, it may have happened because you didn't use your head or didn't think about consequences. But maybe you were completely innocent and the incident was an accident of fate which put you in the wrong place at the wrong time. It may not have been anybody's fault at all. Perhaps the scary thing *almost* happened, and when you realized what may have been–you were terrified out of your wits!

Example

It was another gorgeous summer day for us "cottage kids" at Long Branch on the shores of Lake Ontario. My friends Ed and Clark Girard were ready to jump into the freezing cold lake and spend another day mostly underwater looking for precious rocks or playing water tag! Everything was fine until their mom started hollering at them that they were going to get more ear infections and they had to stay inside and read!

My day was ruined without a friend in sight. Then I got the idea that I could walk to Etobecoke (EE-TOE-BEE-COKE) Creek and see what was cool over there. I think it was the Indian name that made the place sound so unusual and kind of mysterious. I had never been there and barely knew the way. But it seemed like it would make a great story to tell the Girard brothers. Because I was dumb, I hadn't told anyone what my plan was for the day.

When I arrived at the creek, my heart sank. There were a few funny-looking characters hanging out and no small kids my age. It looked like a mud hole with a diving board which I was dying to try. I didn't know anybody, so I didn't care if I looked like a fool doing a belly flop off the board. I had never been on a diving board before, and it was so springy I thought I'd break my neck before I even hit the water!

I did a practice jump and popped up like a piece of bread in a toaster. When I hit the water, I was all out of shape. I couldn't figure up from down when I broke the water and shot down toward the mucky bottom like a bullet.

Collecting myself I started to swim up-up-up frantically. My eyes were wide open and the creek water looked a sickening greenish yellow. I was frightened half to death as I realized that I was running out of air, and I was seized with panic! There was no way to judge how far up I would have to swim to see the sky again. And then I remembered! No one was aware that I was at Etobecoke Creek!

Finally I broke the surface choking and sputtering. My chest was heavy, and I knew for certain that I had come close to losing my life in that murky creek. I vowed I would never tell the story to anyone!

To this day, I can't watch movies with threatening underwater action. It makes my throat close, and my heart pounds with the old fear of drowning!

E. Morris, age 14

Name _____

I Was Scared Silly

Tell of a scary experience you or a friend has had. Did you learn anything?

Great Opening Sentences

Elmore Leonard, a famous author of detective stories, once told his secret about opening sentences. He said that when he started writing a story he tried his best to start his story with a sentence that was a "grabber"! In other words, the beginning of his story was so strong and interesting that it would grab the reader's attention immediately and make it impossible to put the book down! We may not be able to produce such riveting opening sentences as a professional writer, but we can certainly try!

For the Teacher

One of the most famous opening sentences to a story was written by Edward George Bulwer-Lytton in 1830 in his novel entitled *Paul Clifford*. In its entirety it reads:

"It was a dark and stormy night and the rain fell in torrents, except at occasional intervals, when it was checked by a violent gust of wind which swept up the streets (for it is in London that our scene lies) rattling along the housetops, and fiercely agitating the scanty flame of the lamps that struggled against the darkness."

An Exercise with the Entire Class

**Finish these opening sentences with a colorful idea;
then read the ones that follow below.**

1. It was just one of those days when . . . (everything went wrong . . .).
2. Halloween is on its way and I . . . (am going to dress up as a hot dog).
3. She was wild about magic and learned to . . . (pull a rabbit out of a hat).
4. Would you believe that my dog . . . (sings along with country western music on TV)?
5. In the old days kids sat around the radio and (used their imagination).
6. Soccer may be the world's most popular sport but . . . (give me basketball any old time).
7. When the faculty played basketball against the students, it was . . . (the funniest thing that happened at school all year).
8. Smells coming out of the kitchen were like heaven when (Mom made meat loaf).
9. Who could be out digging in the garden on such a . . . (miserable, dark night)?
10. A shadowy figure was seen against the green glow of the computer unaware that (detective O'Reilly was watching every key stroke).
11. My Dad didn't like my friend because . . . (she never spoke a word).
12. They started to fight on the playground when we . . . (talked them down).
13. This tough kid surprised us when he . . . (started to cry).
14. Cool music started in the gym and the shy kid . . . (slipped out of the exit door).
15. When he got his license to drive, . . . (he was a changed person).
16. If I could eat a meal in heaven, . . . (it would be pizza).
17. She just didn't fit in anywhere until . . . (she stopped acting like a goof ball).
18. Danny was a very short fellow but was determined to be . . . (a hoop star).
19. Sometimes on a freezing cold winter night, I . . . (think about the homeless).
20. The advertisements screamed, "We can change your life! Win a million dollars!" so I . . . (turned the page).
21. If you really care about the environment, you will . . . (learn more about recycling).
22. We called him "the lone stranger" because . . . (he rode a horse into town).
23. When I got the job at Burger Barf, I was thrilled with . . . (my first paycheck).
24. The strong, smiling soldier walked into the first grade classroom, but you could tell that the little kids . . . (scared him).
25. He huffed and he puffed and he (blew the house in)!

Assignment

- Each student will write an unfinished opening sentence on a slip of paper. Fold the papers and put them in a hat. Pass the hat around so that each student will take one. Read the partial sentence aloud, and then finish it for the class to hear!

- In the opening sentences above, stop *in a different place* than indicated. How does that change the finished statement? (It adds even more variety.)

- Try finishing an opening sentence and then ask for a volunteer who is willing to tell the entire story !

In an exercise like this there is an infinite number of story possibilities. What does the word *infinite* mean? (Having no boundaries or limits!)

Great Opening Sentences

Now it's your turn to find interesting opening sentences. Look through books, magazines and newspapers. List opening sentences that appear to be interesting or unusual to you. Read your favorite one to the class.

Nutty News I Have Read

Sometimes you read or hear about a story in the news that is so funny or weird that it is hard to believe it really happened! Be on the lookout for such a story or ask someone at home if he or she has a memory of a strange or silly item in the news for you to write about. You may have guessed by now that I, too, have a story that makes me laugh every time I repeat it!*

Monkey Business

There is a government agency called the U.S. Fish & Wildlife Agency that has agents who work hard to uphold the laws that protect monkeys! This case was reported by U.S. Attorney Dan Gelber whose agents were in Miami trying to prevent illegal monkey business! They had a plan to trap a certain Director of Zoos who wanted to buy and smuggle two primates across the border. One of the real gorillas was replaced by a U.S. agent who was dressed in a gorilla suit! When the "delivery" took place, the smaller gorilla was so vicious that he frightened the zookeeper with bodily harm. When the "monkeyshines" were over, the U.S. agent stepped out of his gorilla suit and arrested the zookeeper for trying to break the law!

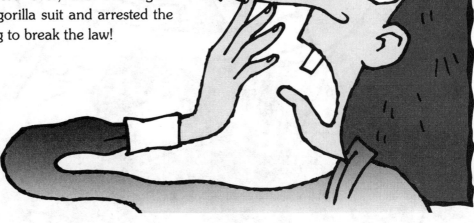

*This old story appeared in *Newsweek* magazine the week of February 8, 1993. It was on page 59 in a feature entitled, "That's Life."

Here is another strange newspaper story.

Only the Hose Knows

On the hottest day of summer one August, Mr. Klutz, a certain householder in Detroit, went out to water his lawn, but his hose seemed to have disappeared. He finally found it lying on the lawn with the nozzle in place. The trouble was that most of the 50 feet of hose seemed to have disappeared down a hole in the lawn. The man pulled and pulled. For a while he seemed to be winning the tug of war, but when he walked away, the hose disappeared again–swallowed up–down the hole. He called his neighbors over who scratched their heads but couldn't offer any solution. Finally the man called the newspapers to send someone out to take a picture of him pulling on the hose unsuccessfully! No one had the answer. Was it a troll? Was it a hose monster? Was it . . .

No one solved the bizarre mystery as far as we know!

Nutty News I Have Read

What strange, silly or weird story have you read or heard about in the newspaper?

Sell That Book

There is a great deal of money and creative energy that goes into the marketing of a book! In the publishing business it is well-known that a catchy title and an attractive book cover are often the hooks that capture the interest of the readers. A capsule review of the content and perhaps an interesting picture of the author on the back cover of the book may be just enough to make a customer buy that book! Some publicity people say that (all together) it takes 30 seconds for the reader to pick up the book, read the "blurb" in back and decide to buy it. As budding authors, it is important to have books in your hands! In this way you, too, can examine the book jackets for details about the book, author, publisher, copyright dates, name of the illustrator (if there is one) and a synopsis! Don't forget the price!

For the Teacher

An excellent example of this lure is the computer book entitled, *DOS for Dummies* written by Dan Gookin in 1991, published by I.D.G. Books in Foster City, California. The response to the unusual title sparked an avalanche of Dummy books on all subjects! As of 1998 the company had 50 million of these books in print!

Assignment

1. You are a big publisher. Give yourself a company name. Make it impressive, funny or interesting. (Kadeckle, Vesper & Croynd)

2. What city and state are you in?

3. What is the copyright date of the book you just published? What is a copyright? (legal protection of a creative work and its profits)

4. What is the author's name?

5. On the back of the book jacket write an interesting biographical sketch of the author and a synopsis of the story to capture the reader's interest. An example follows on page 37.

What Is a Synopsis?

A synopsis is a brief statement which tells what a written work is about.

Example

Pickle Juice by Ima Dill, Delly Publishers, 1600 Roadway, New York, NY 10019.

This is a gripping novel featuring Ms. Pat Strami, our favorite super sleuth, in another suspenseful adventure. She takes us through the back alleys and machinations of restaurant profiteers for whom money and treachery are the bottom line! Helping her along the way are her two loyal companions–her dog Brisket and her muscular sidekick and karate expert, Chop Liffer! In this adventure we follow Pat into the slippery side of wholesale spoiled meats recycled into delicatessens for fat profits! Once again she proves that crime doesn't pay! Another book in Pat Strami's wry style!

The author, Ima Dill, has resided in France where she studied at the Sorbonne and in East Detroit where she graduated with honors from the Institute of Muffler Repair. She is an honored Fellow of the Kay Kaiser College of Musical Knowledge and Storm Door Repair.

Book Reviews

"Ima Dill has nailed the bad guys again!"

"The best writer in crime fiction today!"

"A huge literary talent."

"The work of a powerful imagination!"

"Gritty, tough and a laugh-a-minute!"

Soon available in your favorite bookstore in paperback.

Sell That Book

Did you ever read a book and wish it would never end? What is the title and author of the best book you ever read? Explain what made it so wonderful!

I Need an Invention Because

Did you ever wish that you had some help from a clever source that hasn't been invented yet? When we talk about careers in class, I just get frustrated! How am I supposed to know what occupations are in the world? I'm only a kid! Now's the time for a special personal service that will explore my interests and skills and match me to jobs that would suit me. Would that be wonderful or what?

Example

State Your Problem and Your Wish

Help! My room is a disaster! I need "something or other" to keep my junk straight, my clothes hung up and some kind of organization for my hobbies. I don't mind the mess, but my mother is on my case and keeps reminding me that there is a limit to her patience. I'm afraid that soon she will come in and toss all my valuables out in the garbage. My brother shares my room and he says he can't stand me either.

Another Wish

I love ice skating, but no matter how hard I try, my ankles turn way over and I get shin splints and look like an idiot. I don't want to be a drag on the other kids who are really good. There must be something out there that could help me improve my performance!

Another Wish

Math was really easy for me last semester. This year I was put into "Honors Math," and to tell the truth, I don't know what's going on. It's like I never did a problem before. It is too embarrassing to go to the kids in my class after acting like a genius. My marks are falling into the basement, and I need secret math help–fast!

Assignment

- Describe the problem you want solved.
- Describe what work you want your invention to do.
- Where would it be available?
- Will there be any rules or regulations regulating the use of the invention? Why? Include any other necessary information on your choice.

What could happen if the following items were available?

Add to this list.

- magic glasses
- a cloak that could make you invisible
- a brain booster
- a muscle booster
- a quick look into the future
- a telephone to the past
- machine-altered faces for sale
- free private instruction for any school kid
- instant friends
- a change-of-neighborhood machine
- a genius robot friend
- a personal future forecaster machine (would you really want this?)
- a pillow study machine while you sleep
- an age machine that goes forward or back
- a robot with perfect taste to dress me daily
- a genius pen that could write fantastic plays and stories
- some device to create instant musical talent
- a radar-like screen to reveal what people are really thinking
- a soul mate designator to search the entire world for a perfect mate
- a mechanic who could design a car that was safe and affordable for kids

Questions

1. Is there something on this list you think is wonderful? Why? _____

_____

2. Is there something on this list you think is dangerous? Why? _____

_____

3. Pick an invention and write your reasons for each answer. _____

_____

I Need an Invention Because

Advertise your invention. Give it a name and a price. Explain what it can do. Draw a picture of your brain-child.

It Took Courage

When you think about courage and bravery, it's not always about someone who is big and strong! It's not always about saving a drowning person or rushing into a burning building or fighting in a war! A lot of people have courage in other things in small but important ways. Maybe you have to make a speech in front of your class and that takes courage; perhaps you want to express an unpopular opinion and you know others will disagree but you say what you have to say anyway. Many experiences–small or big–can take courage. Here is an example:

Example

This happened a very long time ago.

I was 12 years old in the sixth grade, and I hadn't been in that school for very long. One day in the social studies class, the teacher started to talk about the workers who were striking at the plant just outside of town. We didn't talk about why the men were striking and picketing the factory. She reminded us that the company paid the workers and helped them support their families. Then the teacher said, "If you think the strikers are right–stand up!"

My father worked in that factory and he was one of the strikers. I knew my dad was a very good man and he must have good reasons for striking. So, of course, I got up and stood by my seat. I was the only one in the entire class who stood up! The teacher looked at me and said, "I think you are unAmerican." My face was burning red, but I knew I had done the right thing.

Name withheld, age 14

You don't always know what takes courage for someone else. It may look like nothing to others who are present at the time!

Example

Told to the author.

Alexander was five at the time. He was all dressed up as part of the wedding party since he was the ring bearer. He was standing in back of the chapel with the bridesmaids waiting for his turn when the flower girl started to get nasty. She told her mom she wasn't going to go down the aisle, and she was really getting mean. She acted tough and threw herself on the floor and started to kick and holler! The grown-ups didn't seem to know what to do with this little brat! Alex started to feel sick to his stomach and didn't know if he could walk down the aisle all alone. One of the bridesmaids took the flower basket quietly and said, "Alex, we must both do our jobs for the bride and groom. You and I must go down the aisle into the chapel together right now–just as you practiced." He had to face all those grown-ups–staring and smiling at him. "The worst thing," he said, "was that I was so afraid that I would burst out crying and people would think I was a baby, too." But he made himself strong and even though he felt "shakey in the knees," he did the job he was chosen to do! When he made it to the altar successfully, he was very relieved and his mother squeezed him and gave him a kiss for acting so grown-up!

Alexander Bryer Lipson, age 7

Discussion

The definition of *courage* is "the state or quality of mind or spirit that enables a person to face fear or danger with resolution, with confidence and with bravery." *Courage* can mean many things.

Can the class think of those situations in every-day life that take guts to face?

A True Story

A boy I know, (who was well-liked by his classmates) was to have given a speech in class as part of an assignment. He asked his teacher if he could get a letter from his doctor stating that he could not give speeches! She said, "No!" When he got up to deliver his speech, he trembled so badly that he had to sit down. For reasons many of us can understand, the effort took more out of him than he could manage!

It Took Courage

Write about a time when you or someone else did something that you thought took courage.

My Best Characteristic

No matter how modest you may be, there are certain personality traits you have that are valued by other people! You may feel uncomfortable about discussing your strengths, but there comes a time when you must admit to yourself, "I am valued by others for a very good reason and that is _____!" Perhaps you are the kind of person who always has a smile and a cheery greeting for everybody; maybe you are right on the spot when someone needs help and doesn't know where to turn; perhaps you always know what to say when someone is depressed and feeling down. Maybe you make others feel smart and good and competent. You may just have that wonderful knack of knowing how to make friends and keep them!

Discussion

- What are the characteristics that you value in other people?
- What traits do you think are especially important in friends?
- If you wanted to improve something about yourself, what would that be?
- Why do people hesitate to point out their strong points?

Example

My most recognizable character trait is that I am ambitious. When I have a task to do I try my best to get it done correctly. When I have a test, for example, I study for it the night before and try to have total concentration while taking it. While I play my musical instrument I concentrate very hard on tone, technique and rhythm. I have many goals in life that I will try very hard to succeed at.

Jessica Vitek, age 13

Example

I know this isn't exactly what the assignment was supposed to be, but I have a hard time answering about my best characteristic. The reason is that some people think I try too hard to please *everybody* and it knocks me out a lot. I am not trying to be better than anybody else; it's just that I can't stop doing what I'm doing. Other people think it's nuts and I should just go ahead and satisfy myself. I still think my best characteristic is that I try to please other people.

Ron Pruette, age 12

Discussion

- Can somebody have too much of a good trait? Explain.
- How can it be harmful to try to please too many people?
- If you were trying to help Ron by writing him a helpful note, what would you say?

My Best Characteristic

What would be the very best compliment anyone could ever give you? Explain.

You Are a Restaurant Critic

Most of us enjoy going to a favorite restaurant for a snack or a good meal. Once in a while you want to try a different restaurant and are curious about the menu, the prices and whether it is "family friendly." Put yourself in the role of a food critic who writes for the *Sanilac Gazette*, a neighborhood paper. You travel around and eat at different restaurants to give your readers a critical report. People read your column and follow your advice. Nobody knows your real identify. (Why?)

Assignment

As a person who travels around to different restaurants, you are especially interested in the descriptions on the menu. Everything that is offered has a fancy name and sounds like it is fit for a king.

Example

Roast beef may be called "Signature slow roasted with an herb crust." Fish may be called: "Delicate lake white fish broiled in lemon perfection sauce."

If you had the job of preparing the menu, how would you describe the menu offerings for:

meat loaf

hot dogs

fish

soup

bread pudding

creamed tuna and noodles

chocolate cake

gelatin

Be extravagant with your adjectives!

Rating Scale

☆☆☆☆   Excellent   Prices: high, medium, low

☆☆☆   Good

☆☆   Fair

☆   Don't Bother

Your Friendly Food Critic

Try the delicious barbecued ribs at the Rib Shack where the ribs are prepared in the big window overlooking Southern Boulevard! People stand and watch the chef baste them until they are brown and well-done. The prices are low and for children under 12, the meals are half price. The barbecue sauce is a little on the hot side, so beware. Try the unusual French fried onion flower and the homemade root beer. The restaurant is bright and clean. The service is a bit slow for hungry diners, but the high school wait staff is very friendly and that makes up for the wait.

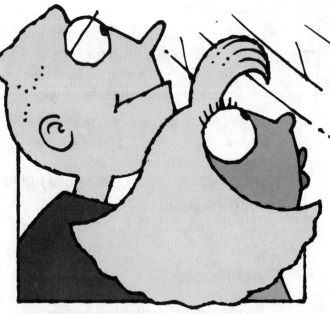

Suggestions for the Critic's Review

- Pizza Palace
- Barney's Hot Dogs
- The Sheik Middle Eastern
- Oceanna Fish Fry
- Peking Inn
- The Farm House
- Enrico's Italian

You Are a Restaurant Critic

Check one.

❑ I do like to eat in a restaurant, and these are my reasons why!

❑ I do not like to eat in a restaurant, and these are my reasons why!

Draw an attractive, overhead sign of a restaurant which you think will bring in customers.

My True Friend

No matter how old or how young you may be, there is nothing like the comfort of a person who is exactly on the same frequency as you. You like the same things, you laugh at the same kind of humor, you give each other warmth and sympathy and honesty and there are no hidden brambles that scratch or injure under the surface. Honesty, affection, loyalty, admiration and respect are part of the friendship package through good times and bad.

Example

My True Friend

I thought a lot about this. I thought about things that my friend and I have done together, about the fact that he is laid back, about how funny he is and how much we laugh together, and things he says that make me feel better about myself. We like the same things like hiking, nature trails and movies that are dumb. We see the world in the same way. It's not always swell stuff between us. I hate it when he tells me things I don't want to hear, like I acted dopey or I was obnoxious or loud–or even that I need to take a shower with a bucket of lye or I had dog breath. But who else would care enough about me to tell me such stuff? I like it that when his family is going to do something cool he always asks if I can go along. He always comes through for me, and I hope I do the same for him. His name is Leo, and he hates it.

Neil McCabe, age 14

Example

True Friends

Some people will think this is strange, but it's true that my parents are my best friends. They are an inspiration to me for being everything in my life. My parents worked hard to get us to live in the United States which is a better place than my native country which is in a war zone. Mother and Father worried about our life and future. They worried about my grandmother, because they didn't want to leave her alone in Iraq. At last when we came here we were all together as a big happy family with eight children. My parents work very hard for their money, but they do not refuse to buy some things for their children to make them happy. They want us to study hard and that is the most important thing. In my Chaldean culture girls are not allowed to have anything to do with boys. My parents don't let me go out with boys, but they let me talk to boys and this is better for me. When I get older, it is unreal to think I can get engaged without knowing boys socially. My parents are everything to me. They are like a gift to me. They never think of themselves, only of their children. I believe they are my angels protecting me from every sad moment, and I am so proud of them.

Athor Mikhail, age 16

Example

This is *not* about a good friend!

My team the Comets was playing against the Red Hots. I did some passing, tough guarding and helping out. We were tied 19 to 19 in overtime. There were several attempted shots by both teams with no success. All at once I realized that no one was guarding me. I thought the ball was going to be passed to my friend Katie, a team hotshot, but instead it was passed to me. I got the ball, moved like a streak and shot. Swoosh! Basket!

I, Nina–Won the Game 21 to 19! We were all in shock, especially me! After I got hi-fives and compliments, I ran over to Mom and hugged her. She was as thrilled as I was! My coach said that he was hoping that the ball would be passed to me and that I would shoot and make it. And I did! Everyone was happy!

The day after the game I was at a Girl Scout meeting with my friend Katie (remember, the team hotshot?). We were there to present a contribution from our troop. It was an honor to do this so I asked if I could be the one to walk to the front with the contribution. When Katie heard me make the request, she leaned over and said nasty-like, "Just because you made the winning basket yesterday doesn't mean you're something special, you know!" I felt very bad. When I told my mother, she said, "A true friend would glory in your achievements."

Nina Cohodes, age 12

Assignment

There is a great deal to be said about the importance of friends and how they make us feel worthy and fortunate. Discuss and list on the chalkboard the important attitudes that you believe nourish a friendship.

Example

- Sharing happy and bad times
- Being a giving person and not a taker
- Being kind and tactful in appropriate criticism
- Accepting differences in personality
- Honoring confidences
- Allowing your friend to have other friends
- Respecting differences of opinion
- Being forgiving and understanding

What are the qualities of friendship you value?

Do you have or have you read a story of friendship that you would like to share?

Note: There are some people who say that their parents are their best friends. And "parents never turn on you"!

My True Friend

Describe your true friend. If you do not have such a person in your life at this time, describe a person who could be a good companion for you.

These Things Worry Me

Authorities on adolescent growth and development know that young people (like grown-ups) must deal with many serious problems and worries that concern them on a daily basis. These issues are as real and as troubling as those which adults must face. Studies reveal that the following list is representative of some of the topics which trouble teenagers:

Examples

Being humiliated
Looking ugly
Sounding dumb
Moving into a new neighborhood
Not being chosen at a dance or on a team
Going blind
Seeing one's parents argue
Fitting in
Being outside an important group
Dressing wrong
Getting decent grades
Earning money
Being cool
Not having any friends
Parent/Teacher approval
Life and death
The environment
Nuclear war

Assignment

Question:

What do you think kids worry about?

Discussion

Some questions and statements to ponder.

1. Can worry be a good thing? Yes, because it alerts you to problems you are facing or which may be in your environment to which you must respond or resolve.

2. If you are anxious about a test, how can that have positive results? (It can motivate you to study.)

3. How is fear a good thing? Fear of something that is harmful moves you to protect yourself. It can prevent you from doing something destructive.

4. What do you do when you worry?

5. What do you do to feel better? Ride your bike, write in a diary or a journal, volunteer to support a cause! (Ask the teacher what she/he does).

6. How can talking to a friend, a coach or a relative make you feel better?

7. Worry calls for problem solving (rather than striking out). Ask questions of yourself: How should I handle this situation? What would be the outcome, depending upon other options?

8. Fear and worry are normal feelings which everyone has. But, are there larger conditions in the world (outside yourself) that concern you? Explain.

9. How do you find solutions? Do you talk with others, examine all sides, try to resolve a situation or just stew about it?

10. Is it hard to decide what is within your control or not within your control? Explain.

11. What does it mean to have power over your own behavior?

12. What fateful things are not your fault? (*Fate* means outcomes, results, events, a consequence or a happening.)

13. We all need help with difficult situations. Who can kids turn to when in distress?

If you agree or disagree with any statement above, write a paragraph expressing your point of view.

Example

This Is What Makes Me Worry

When I come to school I start thinking about going to classes and not being late. I worry about getting good grades, and I worry about being on the honor roll. I worry about answering questions and not feeling stupid. I worry about how long I will feel lonely because there are no other Bengali students in this school. I worry about my family, too. I worry all the time about being successful and about my personal life. I am a strict, observant Moslem from Bangladesh. I don't want to go out with girls until I am an adult. That is my custom and that is what I believe in. But then I worry about what kids in this school will think of me when I don't go to dances or activities like they do.

My health is another concern, because my body is important to me. My good health makes me happy and helps me to work hard and to look cool. Of course I worry about looking cool. I think everybody does. These are only some of the worries which I have. They are enough! Oh yes, this week I am worried about how I am going to do this homework paper on "possessives." Worry never takes a rest.

Mohammed Iqbal Haque, age 15

Example

My Worries About the Environment

I fear that in a century or so everyone and everything in the environment will be destroyed by pollution. If this does happen, no matter what kind of environment one lives in, one would also be destroyed. The way this could happen is this: we pollute the ground. A herd of plant eaters grazes on the polluted ground and plants. The plant eaters start dying because of poisoning. That would leave us foodless. (The ground would be polluted to the point that it would be unfit to grow anything or support any plant life, and the animals that humans eat and use would be poisoned or dead.)

I also fear that we will soon have no forests since farmers in the rain forest still burn, cut and utterly destroy the trees. That is not all. This leaves many animals and plants homeless. More than 10,000 species have already become extinct! The good news is that many people are also trying to **help save our Earth**!

Rachel Rose Lipson, age 9

Worries

These Things Worry Me

What do you worry about, and how do you deal with your worries?

How to Write Dialogue

The word *dialogue* means "a written or spoken conversation between two or more people or a conversational passage which takes place in a play, in a book or in a performance." One of the most common places in which we find dialogue is the comics where the conversation is in the simplest form and the most understandable. Conversation is very hard to write because of the difficulty of capturing how people really speak.

Another important reason that dialogue is hard to write is because the tone of voice, the rise and fall, and facial expressions all help to give us meaning as we listen. In *reading* dialogue, those clues are not there to help us. Here is an example of how many ways in which one sentence can be stated in different ways! The class or individuals can respond depending upon the attitude of the speaker.

Write this sentence on the board to be read aloud: *You really are a rocket scientist!* Now ask for volunteers to read that same sentence given the circumstances given below. The reader must capture the different meaning implied, as the speaker's attitude changes.

How would you say it if . . .

You truly believe your friend is the smartest kid in school. You say, "You really are a rocket scientist!"

You are upset with a kid in school who is as dumb as a door. You say, "You really are a rocket scientist!"

Or

Tiffany walks up to you wearing a new sweater.

You think her sweater is really a beauty, and you say, "Where did you get that sweater?"

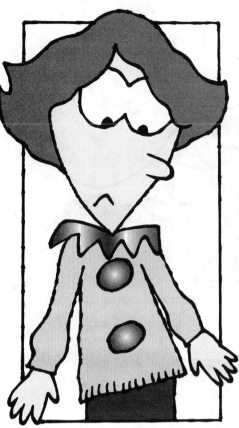

Or

You think Tiffany's sweater makes her look like a clown, and you say, "Where did you get that sweater?"

You use the same words, but you alter the pitch and tone of your voice.

When dialogue is written, the reader must be given more clues in order to understand exactly what is going on! In the comics the pictures give the reader the clues and there is not so much guesswork involved.

There are rules of punctuation for written dialogue in a story. The spoken words must have quotation marks around them. Each speaking part starts with a new paragraph.

Example

Sir Knight wanted to hide his bald head and so he went to a wig store.

"May I help you, sir?" asked the clerk.

"Yes, you may. I want that black, curly one."

"A good choice, sir," agreed the clerk.

The knight tried it on and was very pleased with himself.

"I am rather handsome now, I believe!"

He left the store quickly, mounted his horse and joined his friends. Sir Knight was feeling quite grand galloping along with his black curls bouncing when a sudden gust of wind blew off his new hairpiece in one great swoop! Everyone howled with amusement!

The knight's best friend joined the others in laughter as he commented wisely. "How did you expect to keep strange hair on your head when even your own hair wouldn't stay there?"

Assignment

Another tricky lesson has to do with the use of the word *said*. It would be very boring to keep reading the same word over and over. What other words were used in place of *said* in the preceding selection?

(asked, agreed, commented)

Discuss some other words that can be used instead, in full sentences.

"I know how you feel," he sighed.

"You can't do that here," she warned.

"I am not your friend," he shouted.

Laughing aloud, she chuckled, "You are a funny kid!"

Also Remember

Each time there is a different speaker, there is a new paragraph. In this way you may not always have to identify the speaker because it is apparent on the printed page.

Example
(Read this aloud to the class.)

"Wendell, you must get up, it's getting late."

"But I don't feel good!"

"You'll feel better when you wash up and have some juice."

"No I won't feel better. Juice might even make me throw up."

"If you don't get up now you will never make it to school on time!"

"I don't want to go to school!"

"You have to go to school, Wendell. You're the principal!"

How to Write Dialogue

Cut out a complete comic strip and replace the dialogue with your own words in the balloons provided overhead. Remember, the dialogue in balloons does not require quotation marks.

I Get Mad When . . .

We all have our limits, but some things annoy us more than others! Some people can just shrug their shoulders and say, "Forget it. It doesn't really matter." Perhaps it doesn't matter to them, but it does mean something to you. Have you ever stood at a counter when the clerk just kept helping the adults and acted as if you weren't even standing there? I think that is especially annoying because kids are people too, and they are entitled to the same courtesy as grown-ups! Now that is maddening. Of course, we have to be careful to guard against a bad-tempered response to a lot of situations. We have to learn to control our irritation and not get as mad as a bear at every turn! Some people will speak up, while others will simply turn away. It depends upon your style. You can't make a war zone out of every situation. It's too hard to live like that. Do you have anything to say to any of the following writers?

Example

People who lie infuriate me. *Mad* just isn't the word for it. Stretching the truth hurts everyone. The lies come between friends and abolish trust. I have learned firsthand how much damage lies can do. Vince, my ex-friend, made up rotten stories to come between me and my other friend, Scott. It was terrible for Scott and worse for me. And now Vince lost both of us. The moral of this story is: Lying hurts everyone, including the liar.

Mandy Adkins, age 15

Example

There are many things that make me mad. I don't like it when people refuse to listen to me at all and I have something important to say. I don't like it when someone is telling me what I should or shouldn't do. Especially if those people are not my parents. I don't like it when people criticize me. I don't like helpful criticism or unhelpful criticism, and the truth is that I don't believe anyone else does either. I don't like "rap" music at all. It makes me mad when I have to listen to it constantly from every loud speaker in every car that passes by. I really get mad when I hear the words to those songs. They put down girls and the girls still walk around singing them. It also makes me mad that some kids insist on acting black when they are really white. I get so mad when I hear some pale, brown-haired kid calling another equally Caucasian kid "Homey" or "Homeboy." How dumb. When people assume I am rich because my mother is a doctor that makes me mad. But when some very cute boys call me "angel" that doesn't make me mad at all.

Natalia Baj, age 14

Example

I get mad when my dad makes promises to me and then it never happens. Like when he said he would take me and my friend Chuckie to a special high school basketball game. I did my homework so we could go. We sat in the kitchen and waited for him but nothing happened. Later he said he was very sorry but that didn't help. We were very disappointed. He tried to tell me that sometimes people have to break a promise as if I didn't understand that. He does it all the time and that's what makes me mad. I just won't believe him anymore. How would he like it if I did that?

Jake Pinkert, age 11

Name _____

I Get Mad When . . .

What is one single thing you can describe that makes you mad?

An Outstanding Person

When you think about an outstanding person, it does not have to be a big athlete, a musician, a movie star, an artist or someone who is famous. There are extraordinary individuals among the people you know! Perhaps the person you have in mind does wonderful things for others, volunteers in the community, drives your school bus, is a crossing guard or is even a member of your own family! There are many people around you who do not get recognition, applause or prizes like celebrities do. These are exemplary human beings who are admirable for the goodness of their hearts and for their nurturing and kind contribution to us all. They simply make the world a better, caring place in which to live.

Example

Of all the people in the world, my grandmother Rachel is the most outstanding person I know. Her house is right across the street from school, and that makes it really easy to visit her. I go over to her house on Hart Street with my friends, and she is always ready with good snacks to eat, fruit juice to drink and a big smile for everyone. She can fix things around the house with her tools, and sometimes she uses duct tape. You won't believe this, but she also knows how to fix things under the hood of her car and that is not easy. When I was having trouble with arithmetic, she had a good idea. Together we looked through the sports section of the daily paper for batting averages, wins and losses and other math facts. We even looked at specials in the supermarket to figure out savings with shopping lists. We are now looking at the financial page for more stuff. When I grow up, I want to be smart and helpful like my Grandma Rachel. She is the best.

Ralph Zackheim, age 12

Discussion

Sometimes when you think of an outstanding person in your life, you may consider the word *emulate*.

It means to strive to equal, to imitate, to be as good as that individual!

What are the personality traits you admire in people?

The Most Outstanding Person I Know

Describe the most outstanding person you know and perhaps would like to "emulate." Present your paper to the person you admire.

Start with *In Praise Of . . .*

I Should Have Shut My Mouth

Once in a while, without thinking, something falls out of our mouths that is so dumb or hurtful or private that we wish with all our might that we could take back the words. But once the damage is done, it is hard to apologize. Nothing can change the fact that we were thoughtless and revealed something that would have been best left unsaid. Perhaps what was said was true; perhaps it was just nasty gossip; perhaps it was a secret that you were supposed to have honored. But what would you say to ask forgiveness or explain that you knew instantly that you should have never opened your mouth? What would you say to someone to whom you have caused extreme embarrassment? What is the painful lesson we all learn from such a situation?

Example

It was one of those bright days when everybody on Hart Street was outside. People were tending their lawns; kids were playing and Mr. Franks, our next-door neighbor, was digging in his flowers. Mr. Franks was a nice old guy. He had a headful of white hair and a big mustache to go with it. He was kind to us kids and always talked about how lucky we were to be able to go to Pasteur School on the corner. He was really strong for supporting the school in any way he could!

But I knew a secret about Mr. Franks that I had found out by accident weeks ago. It happened when Sweeney, the postal carrier, walked down the street one day and Mr. Franks called to his wife, Clara, and they sat on the porch and went through the delivered mail together.

"This here's from Bobby Jo, and this is from Jake's Market and this is a postcard from Denny . . ." and she examined everything that had been delivered and explained every piece of mail out loud.

Well, on the day when we were all outside having a good time, there was a man coming down the street carrying political signs. You know the kind you stick in your lawn that says, *Vote for Clyde Croaker*, etc. He went up to Mr. Franks and said, "Would you support my candidate, sir, by putting this in your lawn?"

I was standing right there and could see that Mr. Franks was getting uncomfortable. He looked at the sign for a long time and shuffled his feet around. There was a long awkward silence, then Mr. Franks said, "Well, I just don't know who your candidate is or what he stands for!"

It was then that I blurted it out! "Don't you get it, mister? Mr. Franks here doesn't know who your candidate is 'cause he can't read!" The minute it was out of my mouth I knew I had announced something that was unforgivable. It was not my place to reveal to anyone that this grown man–our good neighbor–couldn't read and probably had tried to keep it a secret all of his life!

Marty Mazak, age 14

Discussion

- If you were in this situation, could you say anything to Mr. Franks at that moment? Explain.

- If you wanted desperately to apologize to Mr. Franks, you would have to write a note in order to choose your words carefully. Just saying "I'm sorry" would not be nearly enough. As a whole class project, construct a truly sincere note to Mr. Franks. Someone at the chalkboard can record this note as it begins to take shape.

I Should Have Shut My Mouth

Describe an embarrassing remark you have heard someone make in the company of others. (Sometimes little kids can say awful things, too!) If you have the courage, describe a foolish remark that you have made.

My Favorite Music Is

One's taste in music can be formed by many factors. You may have a musical family, and perhaps you have listened to music since you were little. Often we are influenced by our friends and the music they prefer. Exposure to the media–radio, television, movies and live performances–also influences us. Generally our tastes vary and are expressive of our moods. If you have a high energy level, you probably enjoy loud and fast music. Age is also a factor since people listen to music for different reasons–to calm them down; to indulge emotions when one is sad, happy, upbeat or nostalgic. Listening can be an aesthetic experience which puts us in touch with the nature of beauty. When you are working and enjoy listening at the same time, it makes it easier for some people to work (though some may require silence). Lyrics, too, are important since they express the poetic aspects of feelings, social messages and the very texture of life. The poetry of song speaks directly to the heart as we listen. Musical tastes can be fluid as we age and change with the times. Religious observance, dancing, singing and storytelling all have roots in the human history of music.

Assignment

How many different kinds of music can you think of?

rhythm and blues	swing	reggae
hip-hop	classical	rock and roll
jazz	new age	acid jazz
heavy metal	country western	fusion
alternative rock	ska	gospel

Assignment

- With a partner or in a group, write some song lyrics and put those lyrics to some popular music. Give the song a catchy title. Perhaps you can enlist the aid of your music teacher for this task. If your lyrics are funny, that is even twice as good! Look at some old songs such as "Darling Clementine" in an early American song-book. Use some of the old music and create new words.

- Find a poem that you think could be put to music.

- Find some lyrics to a song that you think are really dumb!

- Write out the lyrics to a song you enjoy. Print it on poster board. Present it to the class and explain the meaning!

Example

The musical group that I enjoy listening to the most would have to be DMX. They are a rap group that came out not too long ago. The reason I enjoy them so much is that they rap about the truth. Most rappers have not experienced what it is they are saying. Therefore they do not rap from the heart. They do not feel what they are saying. That is what set DMX apart from everyone else. He has been there and experienced what is being said!

Shaun King, age 17

Name _____

My Favorite Music Is

Explain what your favorite music is. You may also express an opinion about your favorite musical group.

Danger! Danger! Danger!
Noise-Induced Hearing Loss

You may think you are indestructible. But guess what? You only have one set of ears and eardrums. Your hearing can be permanently affected by music that is too loud, never to return to normal again. Or you may develop a condition called "tinnitus," in which you have ringing, buzzing or whistling in your ears all the time. Don't boost the volume when you listen. It can destroy hearing which cannot be recovered.

This information is confirmed by abstracts in medical journals in the fields of otolaryngology, audiology, physiology, etc. re: occupational, industrial and recreational hearing loss.

Are Proverbs True?

Proverbs are always fun when you want to say something that fits a situation like a glove. But! What exactly is a proverb? We will define a *proverb* as "a short, popular saying that is used far and wide." A proverb is considered to express a basic truth or a fact which many people generally accept and understand! True or not, proverbs are wonderful and colorful figures of speech.

We have all heard many expressions that are proverbs, such as:

- Don't count your chickens before they hatch. (You can't be sure how things will turn out.)

- The grass is always greener on the other side. (What you don't have often looks better than what you have.)

- Don't cry over spilled milk. (It's over and done with so forget it.)

- Look before you leap! (Be careful before you get into something.)

- Too many cooks spoil the broth. (When people are working together on a project, it can be a big mess.)

- All good things come to those who wait. (If you're patient, it will happen.)

- All that glitters is not gold. (Everything that looks good may not be good.)

- People who live in glass houses shouldn't throw stones! (You have faults like everybody else, so don't criticize others.)

- The pen is mightier than the sword. (Ideas have more power than brute strength.)

- Let sleeping dogs lie. (Don't stir up trouble.)

Assignment

Find some books of collected proverbs, or look in *Aesop's Fables* for some that appeal to you. Try to analyze the content for its meaning. Explain what you think the proverbs express.

Perhaps as a thoughtful person you want to examine and discuss these proverbs without accepting them as the truth. You may discover that you don't agree with them. You may also discover that they sometimes contradict one another!

Example
Too many cooks spoil the broth.

This proverb means to me that if many people are working together on a project, it won't turn out well. I don't believe that because when we work together in our class, there are a lot more ideas that come from everybody in the group than if only one or two people are working alone. People have many different ideas and if we put our heads together, all those contributions help to create a project!

Are Proverbs True?

This is my favorite proverb and here are my reasons for liking it.

If I Could Change Something About Myself

Most people find fault with themselves. Some tall people want to be shorter; some short people want to be taller; those with straight hair want waves; brown-eyed folks want blue eyes; shy people would like to be more outgoing–and the list of wishes, wants and dissatisfaction goes on and on. The truth is we have to come to terms with who we are and how we are perceived by others. We can change some things and cannot change others, but we all go on looking in the mirror and looking inside ourselves! Perhaps it is human to be wishing that some things about ourselves could be different! Think about yourself as a wonderful piece of work because that is the absolute truth of it. Value what you are, value who you are and be grateful for your capacity to achieve a good life! Believe in yourself.

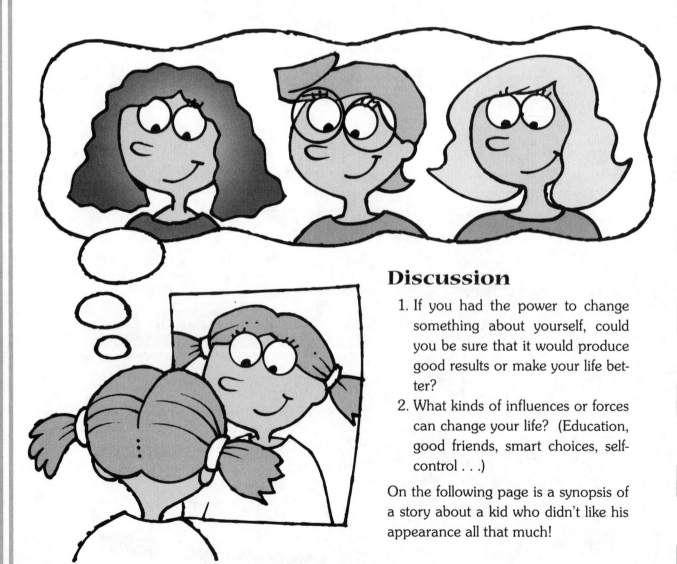

Discussion

1. If you had the power to change something about yourself, could you be sure that it would produce good results or make your life better?
2. What kinds of influences or forces can change your life? (Education, good friends, smart choices, self-control . . .)

On the following page is a synopsis of a story about a kid who didn't like his appearance all that much!

"What Really Counts Is What's Inside You"

Synopsis

His name was Fenton and he was in high school. He had good friends, a brainy girlfriend, cool parents and he did okay in school. But Fenton and his friends were definitely not included in the popular group in school which he called "The Hotshots." One day Fenton saw an ad on a bulletin board in the supermarket. The ad said, "We guarantee to change your looks. Reasonable rates! Apply in person at the TGTBT (Too Good To Be True) Building." The whole thing sounded weird, but the ad said there was no plastic surgery so there was nothing to be afraid of. On the outskirts of town he found the building–a dome-like structure without windows. He thought the whole thing was a bunch of baloney, but he was a curious guy and he went in. No one else was anywhere to be seen–just Fenton and a woman in a white uniform. When he questioned the lady, she said it wasn't a business for profit so it would only cost him two dollars every time he came. They talked about what he could change and at the first visit they shortened his nose while he placed his face inside a plastic enclosure. It was a bit at a time after that–small changes that no one seemed to notice. After a while, some of the kids from "The Hotshots" started to include him in their activities. He no longer saw his good old friends, and he was getting miserable. "The Hotshots" were bubble heads and were only interested in themselves.

On his last visit he learned that the TGTBT Building was closing down. He practically cried as he spoke with the nurse. "You can't leave now. You've changed me, but I'm not happy!" he said. "I have no one to talk to."

As the nurse prepared to leave, she turned and replied coldly, "We promised to change the way you look and we did. Nobody said it would make you happy!"

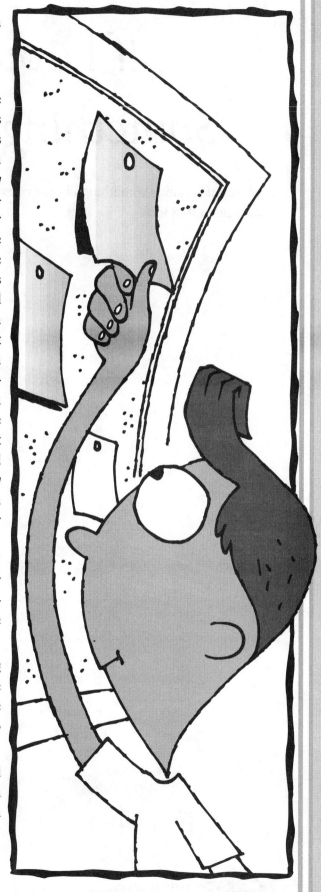

*"What Really Counts Is What's Inside You," from the book *Self-Esteem*, © 1997, Teaching & Learning Company, Carthage, Illinois.

If I Could Change Something About Myself

If you could change something about yourself, what would it be? Or if you are satisfied with yourself, explain that too!

If I Won the Lottery*

Millions of hard-earned dollars are spent on the lottery by ordinary working-class people. The cash prizes are in the millions, and people line up at counters in all kinds of stores hoping that they will win "the big one." There are many choices, all kinds of games and lots of money pours out of people's pockets in hopes of winning a lifetime of easy money. It has been said that (depending upon the numbers of people who participate) you are more apt to be struck by lightning than to win the lottery. But even people who stay away from gambling like to talk about what they would do if they won. Who would be after them to donate money? How would their families react? How much good or evil could the winning do to affect their lives? We do read sad stories about lottery winners who have grief from family and friends because of the money. Winning sometimes brings more trouble than happiness. There are people who make believe they are buying lottery tickets and instead they put the money in a jar for safe keeping. These folks are pleasantly surprised at how much money they have saved at the end of one year.

Discussion

- If it is true that winning a great deal of money in a lottery or in a sweepstakes can truly create serious problems for the winner, how can that be possible? Can you imagine or describe those difficulties?

- Can you share any stories you have ever heard about lottery winners?

- What does this old saying mean: "Money is the root of all evil." Do you agree?

- "There are blessings that money cannot buy!" What are those blessings?

- "A fool and his money are soon parted." How does this happen?

*The Odds on Virtually Everything, Edited by Heron House, New York, 1991.

Example
If I Won the Lottery

I know *exactly* what I would do if I won the lottery. This will surprise many people, I realize, but that doesn't bother me. I have not had a very happy life. My mother died when I was just a baby. I was raised by my grandmother who loved me very much. I had to leave her when my father announced his remarriage. I went to live with my father and his new wife. She never liked me, and I do not get along with her. Sometimes we go for an entire week without speaking to each other. That is just fine with me. People occasionally ask me if I am having a bad day because I never smile very much. The truth is that for me most days are bad days. The happiest moments I have are those I have in the church. It makes me glad just to think about going there. So, if I won a million dollars, I would donate it all to the church. I wouldn't keep a single penny for myself.

Name withheld, age 14

Example

If I won, I would buy a house for my mother and give her many things she has longed for because she has had a very hard life. I would also be generous with my five brothers. The oldest one is quite crazy, and I get furious with him because he never helps me with washing dishes or cleaning house. This is a problem because we come from Iraq where boys *are not* expected to do such things. But we live in America now, and I think we should share my burdens. Even though he gets me so mad, I would get him much basketball gear because he wants to be an NBA star even though he is 17 and is only 5'4"! The twins in our family are in love with the Spice Girls, so I would buy them a poster. My little brother is insane over cars, so I would first buy him a model of a Jaguar. Then I would put money away for him so he could buy the real thing some day.

Emilia Al Hakim, age 13

Example

If I won the lottery, I would buy a bigger house with lots of land for my dog Oxygen, and I'd buy another Boxer so he would always have a playmate. I'd donate some of the money to charities for kids who are sick or disabled and put some money into my mom and dad's RRSP so they could have a better life when they're senior citizens. I'd also save some money so I could go to a very good university and become a scientist. I would give money to my grandma so she can finally quit working and never have to worry about her money for the future. For my sister Madelaine, I'd give her money so she can go to a better university and travel in her gymnastics. One other thing I'd buy is a goalie from the NHL to be my instructor so I can become an NHL goalie!

Daniel Tralman, age 11

If I Won the Lottery 85

If I Won the Lottery

What would you do with the money if you won a million dollars? Whom would you go to for advice?

Junk Food I Love

We are all aware of the effects of poor eating habits. In America, where food is plentiful, there are nutrition guidelines all around us that warn us against the evils of fat, saturated fat, cholesterol, sugar and sodium. On food labels there is consumer information about the contents of products which includes calories and the percentage of ingredients in each serving! Still, no matter how much we understand about bad eating habits, we are lured by all the junk food that is available because–**It tastes so good!**

Discussion

What do you love to eat? When do you eat it? Where? How much? What makes you stop?

Assignment

Bring the wrapper of something you love to eat. As a good research person, list the ingredients which are listed on the package. Does it sound like food? Here is a partial list on the package of my favorite yummies:

> Corn, vegetable oil, partially hydrogenated soybean oil, cheese culture, buttermilk solids, whey protein, monosodium glutamate, disodium phosphate, lactic acid, enzymes, disodium inosinate, guanyate, citric acid, artificial color . . .

A Group Effort for a Product Campaign

Working in a group, put yourself in the roles of scientists working for a snack company. You have access to unusual (never heard of before) chemicals in order to produce delicious snacks. What chemicals are you using?

Grobnick's Gripper Snacks Example

Ingredients (made up from your imagination)

> Grapholinnia, excerbia root, calafragness extract, occidental diaphonous, zarkoff effluvia, tincture of scappula, bargoficus, noxzemia, avunculate oil, essence of salami, yellow food coloring (for buttery appearance).

Directions for Preparations

Extrude onto oven planks. Paint with rainbow streaks. Slow bake this noodle product. Package in deep orange cellophane bags with sunshine and corn-on-the-cob pictures! Print suggestions for dip recipes.

- Let your imagination run wild and do give directions on how to mix, combine and produce your snack.

- Please name your product and suggest a retail price.

- Make a plan for an advertising campaign which includes:
  - a logo
  - magazine pictures
  - a catchy slogan
  - a singing commercial
  - a special toy

Include anything else that will interest consumers (especially kids) and make them want to purchase and eat your product. Create a demand!

Junk Food I Love

We all agree that junk food is not good for you! But if you were in the make-believe city of Egabrag, you would soon discover that junk food there is considered healthy! Describe what the Egabrag folks eat for breakfast, lunch and dinner. (For a clue, spell the city of *Egabrag*, backwards!)

My Favorite Holiday

In every country there are days of celebration! We stop from our daily activities to observe holidays which may be religious, secular or historical. Such observances fulfill the human need to celebrate our membership in the culture, to commemorate and to enjoy good times! Along with the observance of these special days there may be rituals, services, parades, specialty foods, greetings and other customs that characterize the holiday.

Some Holidays in Alphabetical Order

April Fools' Day
Arbor Day
Christmas
Cinco de Mayo
Columbus Day
Earth Day
Easter
Election Day
Father's Day
Flag Day
Groundhog Day
Halloween
Hanukkah
Independence Day
Labor Day

Mardi Gras
Martin Luther King, Jr.'s Birthday
May Day
Memorial Day
Mother's Day
New Year's Eve and Day
Passover
Presidents' Day
Ramadan
St. Patrick's Day
Thanksgiving Day
United Nations Day
Valentine's Day
Veterans Day

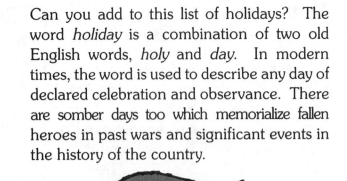

Can you add to this list of holidays? The word *holiday* is a combination of two old English words, *holy* and *day*. In modern times, the word is used to describe any day of declared celebration and observance. There are somber days too which memorialize fallen heroes in past wars and significant events in the history of the country.

Assignment

Create a holiday from beginning to end! It is your responsibility to write a proposal to submit to the City Council. Be persuasive and strong in your recommendation for this new, exciting holiday.

- What is the purpose of the holiday?
- What date will it fall on?
- How will it be celebrated?
- What foods will be featured?
- Will there be any costumes or banners?
- Will it have historical importance?
- Will it include *every* citizen in town?
- Will banks and schools be closed?
- Who will officiate?
- Who (if anyone) will give speeches?
- How will you advertise?
- Who will provide the funds to make this work?

Example
My Favorite Holiday

Thanksgiving is my favorite holiday because all kinds of people in America can celebrate it. Sometimes I hear people talk about being left out of religious things, but this is one time that everybody in the country can have a good time. All you have to do is prepare a big meal (usually a turkey) and invite the whole family. If you don't have many relatives in your family, then invite some people who are alone. They would like that a lot. Maybe if you come from a foreign country and live in this country now but you are maybe a Hindu or anything like that you can do it because now you're here and everybody enjoys a good meal. Maybe you can find out about the Pilgrims. Everybody is welcome.

Billy Boitkus, age 10

My Favorite Holiday

What is your favorite holiday and what are your reasons?

I Had a Strange Dream

Everybody dreams! The subject matter of those dreams can be strange and surreal (expressing the workings of the subconscious mind)! Dreams are a rich source for writing because it is as though your mind is at work and you are simply lending your brains out for that time without any control! They are the stuff of ideas and adventures that we may never experience when we are awake (Thank heavens!). Lots of people experience the same kinds of dreams with their own personal imprint, such as falling, driving and phoning dreams (where nothing works).

Example

Flying

My personal favorite dream is flying! The trouble is that at the beginning it is wonderful as I swoop over the city. I recognize how a bird must feel with the energy to stay on the air currents. The wind makes my clothes billow out, my hair is wild and my sense of freedom and speed is amazing. I don't know where I am going, but it is pure fun. But then something happens. I seem to be running out of fuel! I am flying lower and lower. I am losing altitude. The trees and rooftops are getting so close that I can feel my knees and feet scraping over objects. I realize that I am about to hit the ground, and there is nothing I can do about it, because I am definitely not a bird. The fun is over! I waken before the crash.

Char Snow, age 10

I Am Lost

It feels like I am in a strange city. I recognize the supermarket and the movie theater and some of the shops, but the rest doesn't look like my town. I think my house is somewhere close, and I am embarrassed because I don't remember my address. I wish I had written it down. As I wander around, I seem to be moving farther and farther away from my destination. I try to record landmarks in my brain, but it doesn't help. Then something dumb happens as I go in and out of buildings because I recognize this part of the dream, and I say to myself, "Oh no. Not this again!" Pretty soon I am in a place that looks like a basement or a warehouse, and no matter how many steps I take up and down, there is no way out! Sometimes there is no exit at all. I hate this dream!

Harry Wolok, age 11

Discussion

Share a strange dream with your class.

- Have you driven a car in your dreams?

- Fallen from a great height and found yourself toppling out of bed?

- Have you been starving hungry in a big field, sitting at a table with a checkered tablecloth eating fried chicken?

- Have you tried to phone home, but you can't make a connection because of technical problems?

- When you were little did you dream of scary creatures in your closet, under your bed or floaters coming through your window?

Assignment

Consult your school or local librarian for books for little kids that have to do with the subject of dreams and frightening creatures skulking around at bedtime. Bring these books into class to read aloud. Write a similar book full of the fantasies little kids experience when the lights go out! (Perhaps you remember some of your own!)

I Had a Strange Dream

Dreams and nightmares can be illustrated with art that is wildly imaginative. Describe a dream you have had, and draw a realistic or a free-form picture of the dream. Give your picture a title.

A Science Fiction Adventure

Science fiction is a form of literature that deals with the technical advances of science–past, present and future–in a make-believe story form. It also deals with other wordly events that for us, at this time, transcend possibility. Sci-fi writers speculate about the future in fantastic ways. Sometimes the inventions in these stories come true many years after they are written! In 1870, the author, Jules Verne, wrote *20,000 Leagues Under the Sea.* The story featured a submarine when there was no such vessel as we know it today! He also wrote, *From the Earth to the Moon*, when there was no such thing as space travel! Early authors such as H.G. Wells, Isaac Asimov, Ray Bradbury and Arthur C. Clarke spin their imaginary plots in thrilling and chilling ways.

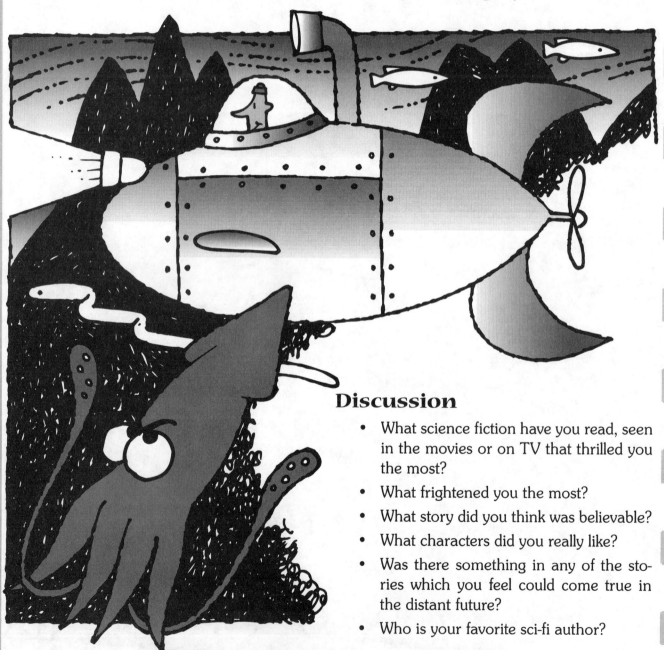

Discussion

- What science fiction have you read, seen in the movies or on TV that thrilled you the most?
- What frightened you the most?
- What story did you think was believable?
- What characters did you really like?
- Was there something in any of the stories which you feel could come true in the distant future?
- Who is your favorite sci-fi author?

Example

The Trip

It was absolutely true–what people said about me, Marty Goober! I could get so lost in thought that I would sometimes lose my way, even on the walk to school. It was one of those drab overcast days, and as I took my usual shortcut through Pinsky's woods, the fog creeped up and surrounded me, swallowed in a pocket of mist. The dampness forced its way through my thin jacket, and I began to shiver. I stopped to get my bearings–turning, turning and looking skyward hopelessly. I was without a clue. It was soon clear to me that I had really lost my way this time. I tried to control my confusion and continued to walk until . . .

Assignment

You fill in the following information.

- If this is a science fiction story, Marty can go back to the past or ahead to the future. You decide which way he goes.

- Describe what he sees.

- Is he on the planet Earth or did he cross over?

- Describe the surroundings.

- Describe one frightening or strange incident that happens to Marty.

Some Possibilities

- Marty seems to be in the future.

  – As the fog clears he is in a shining stainless steel city.
  – The people have no hair.
  – The people live underground, and there is no natural light.
  – The transportation system whizzes overhead on gleaming steel supports.
  – There are no trees or grass that he can see.
  – Everyone is in uniform and all look alike.

Or . . .

- Marty seems to be in the past.
  - The people look like poor hard-working farmers in rough clothing.
  - They look at him curiously.
  - They are fascinated by his watch, radio and earphones!
  - They don't seem to know what his books are for.
  - They touch the pens stuck in his pocket!
  - Nobody speaks and some of them cover their eyes.

Sometimes you do not need a "bridge" that will take you from what is real to the imaginary world of science fiction. Often the setting is the world as you know it–in which something other world-ly takes place. My favorite example of this process is a story entitled, "Lose Now, Pay Later" by Carol Farley.*

Synopsis

Two girlfriends were taking a shortcut through the mall when they noticed a little store that had just moved in. In the display window there was a sign that said *Swoodies*! They didn't know what Swoodies were, but the place was so new and attractive, they wandered in.

There were no customers and no salespeople so the girls took their time. The delicious Swoodie flavors were posted on signs. Best of all, everything was absolutely FREE! Was the store run by machines? They pressed buttons on the vending machines according to directions and from each came a wonderful soft confection in a cup.

They told other kids to visit the Swoodies store. Soon there were long lines waiting for these free treats, but there was a problem! Everyone was gaining weight! Then another business arrived called Slimmers. For a price per pound, a silent attendant helped you step into a machine that took off your fat in seconds. With the loss of 10 pounds the attendant would make a blue mark on your wrist. There were many blue wrists around. Still no one questioned this whole crazy business.

Only little brother, Trevor, wouldn't go near the Swoodies store or the Slimmers. He was sure aliens from outer space were using the human fat as a source of energy!

From 2041: Twelve Stories About the Future by Top Science Fiction Writers, © 1991, Delacorte Press edited by Jane Yolen.

Sci-Fi Adventure

Develop an opening scene that can lead into a science fiction story. (If you like, make this part of a "pass-round story" to which other authors can add!)

A Science Fiction Adventure

Random Stories

If you are having trouble making up a story and searching for ideas, here is an old technique that will help you develop a story no matter how hard the task seems to be. This technique gives you a beginning, a middle and an ending of your choice! Students will work with pencil and paper at their desks to get the sense of this enterprise. This is how it works.

With the Class

Write the lists at your desk as the teacher records on the board.

A. Write the names of five good folks (male or female).
B. Pick five possible places for a story. Write them down.
C. Decide on five bad people. Write them down.
D. Decide on five problems. Write them down.

For item A above, list five good guys (class choice together).

1. Handsome Harry
2. Doris Darling
3. Sweet Sue
4. Mellow Mark
5. Wanda Wonderful

For item B, list five places for a story (class choice together).

1. In a cave
2. In a frozen meat locker
3. The gorilla shelter in the zoo
4. The fun house at the fair
5. A robot factory

For item C, list the names of five bad guys, male or female (class choice together).

1. Sam Slime
2. Rhoda Rotter
3. Cunning Carl
4. Sneaky Sally
5. Buster Brute

For item D on the previous page, list five problems or conflicts (your choice).

(As before, write them down.)

1. Locked in a cage
2. Tied down
3. Pushed into a vat of gravy
4. Lost in a wind tunnel
5. Chased by wild dogs

Here is a way to get everybody's brain in gear! Duplicate the list containing the heroes, villains, settings and conflicts. Give everyone a list in order to construct a random story. Move from student to student and create a story orally from the choices on the list! Make your connections to build a story! Be brave! It can be a lot of fun!

Example

First Student

Handsome Harry was the best mechanic in town. Everybody liked him because he was really clever.

Second Student

Harry worked **in a robot factory** in our town. The robots came off the production line just like automobiles. The amazing thing was that the robots looked just like people!

Third Student

One day **Sneaky Sally** decided to make trouble for Harry. She was jealous because everybody liked him. She caught him napping at lunchtime, and she pulled him up onto the production line where the bolts and screws were pounded into the robots!

Fourth Student

Harry woke up to find that he was **tied down** as the clanking machinery started moving him forward toward the powerful drill press . . . . (The ending is up to you!)

You May

- Use the same list over and over again with a different story each time.
- Increase the lists to 10 times each.
- List any other condition to factor in.
- Have each student put together his or her own story alone at the desk.
- Calculate mathematically all the choices this technique generates.

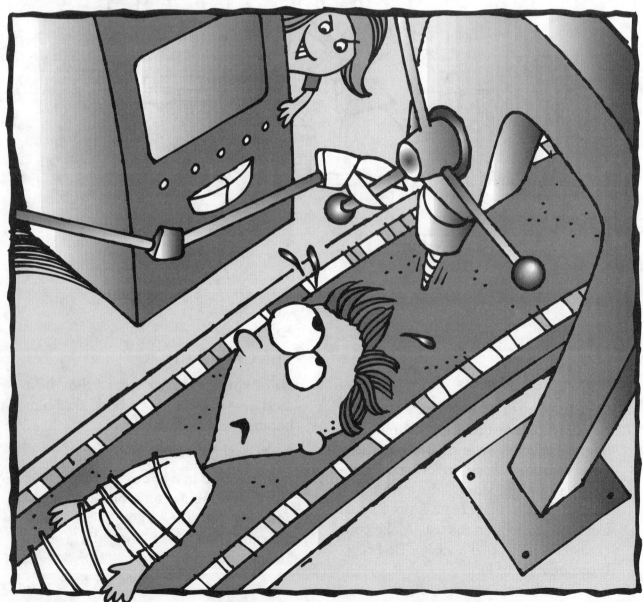

Random Stories

You may try a solo effort using this "random story" strategy. Use the lists from class.

Dear Board of Education

It was a strange assignment, but it was time the students understood the role of their Board of Education. The class interviewed the seven elected members and asked all kinds of questions. They learned that the board members serve for four years. Among their responsibilities, the board hires the superintendent of schools, approves the yearly budget and controls district policies. The members decide whether the district needs additional construction millage money and becomes involved with the community to advertise and support other endeavors that enhance the school district. The students were invited to attend any of the two meetings held each month and were surprised to hear that at the meetings there was always time reserved for anyone in the audience who wanted to speak to the board (regarding relevant interests), even if that person did not live in the district! One of the kids asked, "What does the Board of Education do when someone makes a complaint about a teacher, a student or a sticky situation at school?" The answer was that such day-to-day problems are always the business of the principal and the school administration. The kids were invited to attend any meetings or write to the board about anything that interested them. Everyone was satisfied that they had learned something that day.

Assignment

Back at school the teacher asked the students to write a "positive" note to the Board of Education on any subject relative to school. The following is such a note:

> Dear School Board,
>
> My math class is the most interesting thing on the planet. We cover the most fascinating things like adding and subtracting fractions. My teacher never says a boring word. As we sit through our lectures on how to subtract fractions, we never say a word because we might disturb the people who are paying attention. As you can see, we all love math class and want to be teacher's pet! Even though we all are her pets, we always fight about it. Now it is time to go back to math–so see you.
>
> Sincerely,
>
> Rebecca Lewis

(Of course this letter was never sent, but it is a perfect example of irony. The definition of *irony* is a statement that is made which is actually the opposite of what is meant. It is clear that Rebecca can't stand her math class.)

Assignment

Your school buildings are very old. Your parents and the residents in your district will be casting a vote for or against an increase in taxes for school repairs. You are preparing banners to encourage a vote in favor of that increase. What would you print on the banners?

Name _____

Dear Board of Education

Write a letter to your board of education. You believe there is a problem which deserves attention! The problem may be regarding school policy, lunchroom food, attendance, busing, homework, dress code or whatever is bothering you. The letter must be respectful.

I Was Proud When . . .

When you feel personal pride over an achievement, it means that you have a strong sense of your value. You experience a special awareness and the pleasure of satisfaction from a job well done. Pride does incredible things for your self-esteem. Now and then we all need to enjoy the uplifting of our spirit and morale. We can include all kinds of things that give that special feeling, such as passing a test, winning a game, giving a speech, writing a prize essay or any number of things that make you reach for success! Pride is not just about yourself, but also embraces many other people and events. You may be proud of your country, your parents, brothers and sisters, a friend, your teacher, your class, your team, your school and even your dog!

Discussion

- Pride may not always come from large accomplishments! What has happened in the course of your daily life that has given you pride?

- Describe a time when you were asked to do something that made you feel grown up and capable.

- How can pride have a meaning that is not so positive? (If pride makes you arrogant, a know-it-all or "too big for your britches," that is not a good thing as in "Pride goeth before a fall.")

Example

As the bottom of the final curtain touched the stage for the final time, a rush of pride and adrenaline raced to my already pounding heart. I stood up and laughed while clapping and yelling with joy. The show itself went beautifully, without flaw, and the last note of the last song resounded confidently throughout the auditorium. I had worked on this show for months, and it was all for this moment, for the applause, for the standing ovation, for the elation and for the awed "wow." But to receive these treasures I had to compromise my social life and some academic habits and devote myself to the only completely student-run show at my school. This dedication, along with late nights and hours of phone conversations, was all worth the time, work and frustration for that surge of pride, the feeling that I actually created something amazing and wonderful that people wanted to see. I had done something well and would do it again to have that happiness.

Sarah Cohodes, age 15

Name _____

I Was Proud When . . .

Describe something in your life that made you proud.

Afterword

There was, for me, a lingering sweetness when I came to the last topic in this book and the last reflections from the school kids who wrote with so much feeling. In case you wondered about it, the examples that were used were all authentic experiences! Some students wanted their names used and others did not. And still, some of the names are nom de plumes (pen names)!

But overall, their honesty and earnest effort far exceeded my expectations. At times I was surprised by the sheer volume of what they had to say. At other times the writing came slowly! Those were the moments when teachers used my favorite opening remark: "Talk to me about this . . . ."

The kids had introspective things to say because we tried for topics involving the main themes of their lives. Much of their commentary made me smile (or even laugh out loud), but it was all part of the wonderful harmonics that came from the effort. Here was a chance to explore their personal values and interests on their terms. (As a cautionary note: It was never our intention to be intrusive!)

And sometimes the topics were simply frivolous stuff that was fun to write or think about and use a mountain of words!

With collegial good wishes,

Greta

Greta Barclay Lipson, Ed.D.